GEOFFREY TREASE

GEOFFREY TREASE

Geoffrey Trease

A WALCK MONOGRAPH

by

Margaret Meek

HENRY Z. WALCK, INCORPORATED
NEW YORK

For
IAN MICHAEL
and the students at the
Royal Fort

Library of Congress Catalog Card Number: 64-20834
© The Bodley Head Ltd 1960
First American Edition 1964
Printed in Great Britain

CONTENTS

1. Introduction

Nothing is so characteristic of the English as the way they take important things for granted. Children's reading is a matter of some concern at the present time, and it is fashionable to say that children no longer get the pleasure from reading that their parents did, although hundreds of new titles appear every year, every good bookshop is full of excellent examples of story-telling and the writer's craft, and since the war there has been a publishers' revolution. What is rarely admitted is that when some of the authors, so highly praised by parents in their fifties, were in full spate, the majority of English children were barking at print in elementary school primers. These were the books specially written for children, but they gave no indication that the proper pleasure of reading was other than the relief of word recognition.

So many things have changed in the production of children's books in this century that it is impossible to set a contemporary writer, at the height of his fame and success after twenty-five years of unremitting effort on behalf of writing for children, in a series dealing with his distinguished predecessors, without taking into account how far-reaching these changes have been. We should do the work of Geoffrey Trease less than justice if we thought that he had a broad highway before him when he left Oxford in 1929 and went to London to seek his fortune as a writer. Nor could he then have been attrac-

7

ted to writing for children. This was the period of the Bumper Books, those swollen puffboard monstrosities printed on featherweight paper and judged by their bulk. The influence of the hack writer was at its height. No wonder, then, that those who wanted suitable books for their young still chose Lewis Carroll, E. Nesbit and Mrs Molesworth, or risked Ballantyne, Marryat, Henty and Stevenson. For serious reading there were Scott, Dickens, Bunyan and *The Swiss Family Robinson*.

We have only to look at a selection of titles from the recent *Times Literary Supplement* reviews of children's books to see how far we have come since 1934 when the first Trease novel was published. Now we have children's libraries, with librarians trained to read and discriminate by the standards set by Dorothy Neal White and Kathleen Lines; teachers, whose training colleges are stocked with children's books, are exhorted to know and use the contemporary author; schools are library-conscious, and authors, aware of a sellers' market, produce books to meet every demand as soon as it arises. Then they face the growing discrimination of reviewers.

And the children? Here again we strike a tacit belief that all we need do is to find a good book, put it into their hands and they are readers for life. It is, of course, not so. The revolution has been just as far-reaching in the young reader, and as Trease's stories are bound up with their fortunes and status, it is relevant to mention the most important changes: the development in the concept of reading ability and the increase in educational provision. Since the beginning of the century the belief in the need for functional literacy in the whole community has gradually become axiomatic. This now means more than the recognition of individual words; it takes for granted that reading is an extension of apperception, analogous to seeing and hearing, and that the reader will understand and judge the ideas received and act upon them, or enjoy for himself his own choice of creative writing. This was never otherwise in educated circles, but the extension of secondary education to others besides the middle classes was not something a children's author had deliberately to take into account before 1933. Geoffrey Trease's writing has matured alongside the development of reading habits in sections of the community which have little tradition of literary culture.

This process is by no means complete, and not all children reach the same level of reading ability. A child may have acquired by the age of ten sufficient basic skill to see him through his grammar school career. But what of those for whom reading offers no continuous source of satisfaction, or the others who are variously classified as slow, reluctant or backward readers? On this topic there now exists an immense body of knowledge and authors may be called to account if they concentrate on the literary and gifted child or pay no attention to the needs of a particular age-group. Sometimes they must remind the reading expert that it is by reading books too 'advanced' for them, as well as the bulk of those aimed at their stage of development, that children become both competent and adventurous readers. The modern author must keep free from academic controversy on this subject and insist that his intention is artistic, that his first concern is to write good stories. But if he is totally unaware of the contemporary trends in reading studies, he may find this reflected in his sales.

The intelligent child, on the other hand, reads everything sooner than he once did. He becomes more easily bored with, or rushes quickly through, simple tales of action written for children and moves on to adult stories which have a strong plot action. Hence the continued popularity of Henty and Stevenson. These children are a challenge to the author who finds them stimulating to write for, and many writers now produce books which make demands on young readers as searching as any adult novel. As a result we have a curious paradox, certain children's books are now discussed at High Tables and in Literary Societies. This is all to the good; every art needs its pacemakers.

Writers must also take account of the change in class structure which follows the extension of educational provision, while resisting the temptation to become sociologists and to be drawn into lengthy arguments about whether or not the background of children's stories is that of the upper middle class. There is no doubt that it once was and sometimes still is, but the picture of England that Paul Hazard said he could draw from the background of children's books in 1932 would not be the same one today. A growing class mobility and a heightened class-consciousness are elements a writer cannot ignore if he is to enter the field of stories about children 'just like us'. I once believed that the subtle imaginative process of identification enabled children to leap all barriers between their lives and those of the heroes, but classroom experience taught me that it is easier to make contact with the feudal aristocracy than with children who have expensive holidays.

The amount of time now available for reading 'tales out of school' is less than it was, and only the bookish child who will read even with the television in front of him is the teacher's and the author's delight, for in him they see themselves when young. He is now the exception rather than the rule. For most children reading is agreeable, often exciting, if they find a book they like, and they do it willingly. But it is not the only way to get their vicarious experience, and the interests of adolescents nowadays are active and social. Reading is only one of the many things they do. One knows that it can still confirm and enlarge experience in a way entirely its own, especially in the world of the imagination. But the modern author no longer has a captive audience. He must take time from hikes, clubs, TV serials, dramatics, dancing and idleness. He may succeed in cornering only a part of a dull lesson in class, but when he does, he must make the most of his opportunity and have something worth telling. He has his tricks too, the wily author. His books may be serialised on Children's Hour or on television. The teacher will read out and maddeningly not finish an exciting incident which nags at an exasperated pupil until he has to get the book from the library. The book has to be worth the trouble; it must have something children want, need, or are stimulated by, or else it must not interrupt their games.

This is the situation into which Geoffrey Trease and his fellow writers launch their books. On balance the writers have won. The gloom with which those out of contact with the children's enthusiasm predict the downward trend of reading does not seem to be warranted. Although the hack still lurks powerfully in the undergrowth of weeklies and pulp products, his standards and methods are exposed and ignorance is no longer an excuse for choosing a poor book. The outright purchase of the copyright of children's books has dwindled as a practice, and serious authors expect the same terms from publishers as are offered to other writers.

For twenty-five years at least Geoffrey Trease has been a prime mover in this situation and he deserves more recognition than a short essay can give. I am bound to confess that for years I was aware of his books but never read them; I was the schoolteacher he describes in *Tales out of School*.

' "Have a heart!" I hear some mistress say. "I have had a nerve-jangling day in the classroom, a strenuous afternoon on the hockey field, a row with a colleague and an exasperating five minutes with the Head. Now, having waded through that pile of exercise books, I am expected—this not being a night I have an evening class to take—to spend my last waking hours reading *A Pony for Penelope* or *Mystery at St Monica's*. . . .!" '

But I could not cut myself off from my pupils' enthusiasm, and when in a later pile of exercise books I read something like this, I felt I was being accused. The essay was: 'The Person I should most like to meet.' The writer was nearly thirteen.

'The person I should most like to meet is Mr Geoffrey Trease. He writes exciting history stories and stories about children you can believe in. I wonder why we don't have them in school instead of history books and *David Copperfield*. . . .'

So I read *Tales out of School*, which, although written in 1948 and subject to the same problems of 'dating' as all books on this topic, still presents the most adequate statement of standards in writing for children. Then in a later investigation of how children understand what they read, it became clear that the dichotomy between what-children-like-to-read and what-they read-in-school persists and is strengthened chiefly by teachers and children never finding out what is available. The modern author is the person who can fill the gap, and if we are to make a literate generation of the children in school at present, we need him to help us. Indeed we shall not do it without him. Classics will come, but not by being harped on as the books children *ought* to read. If they are not to be in perpetual opposition to comics, we must understand what the children's author is trying to do.

Since the publication of his first book in 1934, Trease has been quite clear that a children's author is an artist in his own right. This seemingly obvious definition of his role is not always accepted. As a nineteenth-century moralist, an author could claim that the enjoyment of his books was in evil punished and virtue rewarded. Sometimes a lady authoress strayed near the edge with the raptures and roses of vice, but the rue always followed. They were succeeded by writers who set about telling a tale first, and their books for adults were seized on by boys in search of adventure and heroes. Then Marryat, Ballantyne and Fenimore Cooper realised that boys must have their own books and set about telling them stories, so that by the beginning of this century the writer for boys was a definite literary figure.

Why did he not remain so? First because the formula was easy to follow, and this discovery was accompanied by a false belief that whatever is done for children is easier to do. Simpler vocabulary, thinner plots, less attention to accuracy and verisimilitude were the chief features of later adventures. Children who never get good books really do enjoy the bad ones, so the less scrupulous publisher and the hack writer and all the *commis-voyageurs*

14

of book production increased the trade which flourished in newsagents' shops. These had their own clientele who never saw a real bookshop, and still do not.

Besides a false idea of simplification as the operative concept in providing for children, the notion that children lack *experience* was an unacknowledged preconception before about 1945. The fact is that they do not lack it, but their experience is organised to form a world-picture which differs considerably from that of adults, and which grown-ups speak of over-simply as a childish belief in fairies. Becoming grown-up means rearranging the material of this inner world to adjust ourselves to what we gradually discover to be the facts of the universe. The childhood pattern slips away as the adolescent begins to fulfil adult roles. The successful author presents children with an organised illusion which fits their stage of development, a world in which their experience is relevant. In England this has been done most successfully in a particular kind of fantasy writing, of which *Alice in Wonderland* is the prototype and *Tom's Midnight Garden* the latest example, and in the adventure story, historical or modern. In the first of these, time and place give way to a special mode of what Henry James calls 'felt life', and in the second the illusion depends on the characters being accepted as 'just like us'. At their best they are genuine literary kinds. Suzanne Langer says of them:

'These juvenile stories are most skilful poetic

15

creations. . . . Their magic is fairly easy to analyse, and the analysis reveals what may, in fact, be found in any well-told story—that the fabric of illusory events takes its appearance and emotional value entirely from the way the statements which actually compose the story are worded, the way the sentences flow, stop, repeat, stand alone etc., the concentrations and expansions of statement, the charged or denuded words. The ways of telling make the place, the action, the characters in fiction.'[1]

This is the challenge to the writer. He sees how the illusion is created, and he knows that, for the most part, unless he bores them with generalisation and abstraction, the children will come with him. Does he then trouble to make his writing consistent with any standard of integrity of what is suitable for children and also integral in a work of art judged by adult standards? The children cannot make this judgment, and so many writers have assumed that it need not be made. Geoffrey Trease stands out as the children's author who has insisted that no other standard is appropriate. He tells his fellow authors:

'An artist is what the children's writer *is*—a minor artist, perhaps, but an artist none the less, though other people are slow to admit it. For an artist's function is to interpret life, and though the children's author has certain limitations, he can still perform that function where it is most needed—for who needs the help of an

[1] S. Langer. *Feeling and Form*, Routledge & Kegan Paul, 1953, p. 298.

interpreter more than the boy and girl? It is this status, as minor artists, that we should claim and win in the *next* twenty-five years. (I don't think we have it now)—but before claiming it we must earn it.'[1]

I am persuaded that Trease has more than earned the status he claims. Since the appearance of *Tales out of School* in 1949, and Kathleen Lines' *Four to Fourteen* in 1950, it has been impossible for a children's author who has sought recognition for his work to adopt lower standards. This also makes it the more interesting to see how Trease's work has measured up to his own rules and how far his books owe their success to their embodiment of his demands. Artistic integrity is an uneasy bedfellow with economic necessity, and it is possible to be idealistic if one is not dependent on a body of sales and a popularity rating. Current demand is a tyrant, and the output of the children's author has always been large. Veracity in history is an expensive business not lightly undertaken; exactness in place description likewise. Like the teacher, the author is earning his bread and butter, and the temptation to earn it with a little less effort is strong for both and by both must be resisted. Children's books pay; there is no point in denying it. But if one ever slips into the fatal thought of 'only for children', one has crossed the line between the writer of integrity and the hack.

Trease has tried almost every kind except the strictly

[1] G. Trease in an address to the Society of Authors, 4th Nov., 1958.

fanciful: adventure story, historical novel, travel book, straight history, review, criticism and radio play. He lectures to children and teachers and speaks generously of his competitors who have, in some cases, surpassed him in the work he inaugurated. In all this he continues to give pleasure to hundreds of children who know his latest books better than those who write articles about them. By his painstaking analysis of the task in hand he has given many teachers, librarians and parents help in asking themselves what they are really doing when they encourage children to read.

11. Early Work

Geoffrey Trease was born at Nottingham on the eleventh of August 1909, the youngest son of a wine merchant, and went to Nottingham High School. As a child he was the gluttonous reader who delights and puzzles the experts, swallowing fairy stories, the weeklies, the *Children's Newspaper*, bound volumes of *Chums* and the Henty hordes without indigestion. At eleven, he tells us, he was 'editing a form magazine running five serials from one term to the next'. Five years later he was editing the school magazine as well as acting, debating and studying the Greek texts which helped him to win his Classics scholarship to the Queen's College, Oxford. This he resigned after a year. His determination to write was apparently stronger than the attraction of Greats, and in London in 1929 life did not have to break through a cloistered academic seclusion; it was all around in a stark form. Trease was first a social worker in an East End slum, then a journalist, and he also taught in a private school. The early thirties were the period of the writer-propagandist, and Trease's early writings, like those of his distinguished contemporaries, show strong left-wing sympathies.

'At twenty I was selling guinea articles to small papers and hawking an unpublishable novel round Bloomsbury and Covent Garden. At twenty-four, all boats burnt, I was trying every market from women's magazines to literary reviews. I had, some time previously, come across Ilin's documentary children's book, *Moscow has a Plan*. The idea germinated slowly, and one day burst suddenly forth, that children's books were not reflecting the changed values of the age. Adult fiction was. Novelists in the nineteen-thirties did not depict war as glorious or the British as a superior race. Children's books had kept the pre-1914 outlook. . . . I wrote to a publisher whose list indicated probable sympathy, and suggested several ideas, one being a realistic Robin Hood story, in which the seamy side of Merrie England should be displayed, and Robin represented as a kind of premature Wat Tyler. . . . The response to my suggestion was of the kind which normally comes to young authors only in their dreams— a letter by return post, saying that the publisher had been looking for someone to do the job for years, and promising to commission the story on a synopsis and specimen chapters. So, almost accidentally, I became a writer for children.'[1]

What began as almost an accident did not continue as a second-best bet. In fact it was clear that to pay one's way one avoided the children's market. The challenge lay in that 'children's books *were not reflecting the changed values of the age*'; Orwell's version is: 'the clock had stopped at 1910'.

The reviewer of 'Books for the Young' in the *Times Literary Supplement* for August 1930 praised Arthur Ransome's *Swallows and Amazons* as 'unusually inventive and lively'. The reviewer seemed to feel that this was something quite new in that he commended the

[1] *Tales out of School*, p. 26.

'sensible relatives who had enough imagination and self-control to keep out of the way of serious business on the island', but he had nothing with which to compare it.

In 1931 Kästner's *Emil and the Detectives* went unremarked. Notices at this time gave preference to fairy stories, and one detects in the reviewer's tone a feeling of relief that he has to read, not write, these books. A good present for a child was the standard pattern, and the *Monkey Moo Book*, by a fellow of the Royal Society, was recommended as suitable for 'those recovering from spots'. Historical tales occasionally appeared and were praised if they were written in a manner 'which prevents the tale from savouring of the plain history lesson'. 'Children who can still be attracted by stories of the picturesque heroes of olden times will enjoy meeting Hereward the Wake. . . .' The assumption behind this is interesting when one remembers what Geoffrey Trease has done for the historical novel for children. The reviewer's severest stricture occurs in a notice of a 'personal record' of the Great War written for boys. 'There are occasional weaknesses, such as the advice given to boys on their behaviour when in contact with those of birth and education lower than their own.' A story of a modern girl says that she 'found in "good old Britannia" a mother for the one she left behind and was very happy. The book seems to be a record of fact, and is illustrated with snapshots of scenes in London, Bournemouth, Devonshire and other British resorts.'

From our present sophistication it is easy to find this tone inappropriate, this handling inept. It is the more remarkable that Geoffrey Trease saw in this state of writing for children the chance he needed. His first published boys' story, *Bows against the Barons*, appeared in 1934, and is the realistic Robin Hood story referred to in the passage quoted above. Children were quick to grasp the point and the popularity of this early work continued after the war. In the preface to the second edition the author says: 'Boys and girls wrote from many parts of the world. The story was translated into Icelandic, and a friend told me how, when he was fighting in the Spanish Civil War, he found a German translation which had been published in Russia.'

The story is genuine black-and-white. The hero, Dickon, shot a deer after a day of provocation and ran off to Sherwood Forest, where, as in Shakespeare's Arden, we hear of winter and rough weather. The peasantry are oppressed by bailiffs, lords and abbots, squeezed for money, pressed for military service and they can do no more than put up a brave show of revolt. Robin Hood is celebrated not as the stereotyped romantic hero, but as someone who 'dreamed when the rest of us couldn't see further than our noses'. The heroic ideal shines through an impression of lurking danger. Children enjoy and respond to the clear-cut issues of right and wrong. At this time Trease believed that it was his duty to be a propagandist of social and political realism in opposition to those writers who trafficked in improbability. We find his villains capitalist in utterance, and the heroes are the downtrodden proletariat of the thirties rather than twelfth century peasants, but as an example of shaking up the mixture and telling a clear yarn it has still much to offer.

Trease is not without his debts in this and later books to the writers of the late nineteenth century who were sound plot artificers and purveyors of one genuine thrill per chapter. Stevenson showed how to shape an episode and to fashion a climax. He has insight into the fascination of a character like Long John Silver, the rogue who wins admiration 'as original as sin'. Teachers have never worried that the Treasure Island expedition was 'launched by greed and decorated with murder and treachery and concluded with luck rather than righteousness'.[1] Marryat had taught Stevenson that the real world captivated men and boys, while Ballantyne, Cooper and Kingston extended the frontiers of adventure, and morality had to take its chance with the tale. Above all, Henty carried the cult of 'manliness' through nearly seventy books of considerable length, and his present revival is no accident. Dorothy Neal White says that an analysis of the reasons for the survival of these writers would throw light on the popularity of Geoffrey Trease.

We have already hinted that boys want grown-up tales (but not modern adult novels), where the element

[1] Harvey Darton, *English Children's Books*, Second edition, C.U.P., 1958.

of plot suspense is strong. It is a taste which persists in readers of detective fiction, although there intricacy of motive supplants action. Also, I wonder if the movement towards the perfect satisfaction of children's reading needs, the very appropriateness of the books now written for them, makes the danger of 'suitable' reading becoming yet another stereotype. The very incongruities of Henty and Jules Verne are attractive; they have the quirks and quiddities of real, not manufactured style, however peculiar. They make reading memorable, and for some children this is more enticing than the merely suitable.

This memorable quality the writers of the thirties failed to borrow from the major writers of boys' fiction. Harvey Darton says that at Henty's death half the juvenile publishers in London were advertising his successor, so clearly was the market stabilised. An idea of what these books did *not* provide, namely, a vivid picture of the active lives of boys and girls who became absorbed in special pursuits, brought fame and fortune to Arthur Ransome. Now the tide turned, and a new *genre* besides school stories and adventure appeared. Realism came to stay in a cloak of authenticity. With the exactness of a sailing expert and the economy of an artist, Ransome wrote of actual children in the place of swashbuckling prodigies. The illusion is created by loving attention to detail, a technique as old as *Robinson Crusoe*, and its very success makes it a strong temptation for the imitator and publisher of stereotypes.

Trease grasped the appeal of realism and the effect of the adult story for boys. He next tried a school story. *The New House at Hardale* appeared in the *Boy's Own Paper* in 1934, and in book form as late as 1953. The author says he was 'varying an old formula', but the variations extend beyond the limits of Gunby Hadath, although the familiar ingredients of house spirit, no smoking and rugger are all there. The theme concerns an attempt to make a new house out of all the individualists and misfits from other houses and touches some of the springs of what makes a community. Hard work, training and not taking offence are advocated. The characters have a kind of gentle earnestness which Trease's competence in handling the rougher side of school saves from seeming 'soft'. The masters are not blind nincompoops, but responsible adults who judge the facts of a case as they emerge. Those who let the house down are slack and selfish but not vicious. The dialogue 'dates', but this serves to point the difficulty of writing about young contemporaries. The 'bliss' of study tea remains in the school story long after Trease would have cut it out.

The school theme allowed for few variations, for the pattern was confined at that stage to the boarding school. (Other kinds were in the famous education reports which preceded the Act of 1944.) Mystery stories were fashionable, and Trease wrote several before his first adult novel, *Such Divinity*, was published in 1939.

Real progress seemed to be along the way of *Bows against the Barons*, in historical fiction which told a rattling good story and yet did more. The time dimension, the significance of past events, and above all, the involvement of the modern child in the past, would give depth to the adventure story and take it out of the region of sub-journalism. In *Comrades for the Charter* (1934) and *The Call to Arms* (1935) the propagandist element survives. These books are still of interest, for they are the first to treat historical themes from a viewpoint other than that of the establishment. Nowhere in history stories before Trease do we find any indication of what stirred up Englishmen, generation after generation, not always unsuccessfully, to assert that they were men with sovereign rights. What could appeal more to adolescents in their attempts to find themselves? Why, after all, should political consciousness be approved of in children's books only if it is the conservatism of Captain Johns? I am sorry that Orwell does not seem to have known *Comrades for the Charter*, the climax of which is the armed rising at Newport. Trease says of it:

'The general atmosphere of the 1930's gives a somewhat anachronistic flavour to this book. Too many phrases recall the *Daily Worker* of the 1930's rather than the Chartists of the 1830's. I knew very little English history in those days and shudder now to remember the blissful ignorance in which I wrote. Also, I believed in propaganda for even young readers. Now, and for many years, I have held that a children's writer should have the same sort of professional ethic as a teacher—whatever his personal beliefs, he mustn't use his position of professional advantage to press party politics on readers too immature to argue with him on fair terms. This is a difficult issue to live up to, sometimes because of the child's natural preference for black and white characters and clear-cut issues.'

Later books give arguments for both sides, as we shall see, but right from the start the attraction of history is in live issues, involvement, commitment, which alone, we are told, will save us from the sensationalism of the candy-floss world which Richard Hoggart describes in *The Uses of Literacy*.[1]

Commitment also means 'no writing down'. A system of adult values must operate. Recall again the tone of *The Times* reviewer. What self-respecting craftsman wants his work to be thus spoken of? The children's response was forthcoming, but a writer needs the criticism of his peers. How were they to be made to see that in the tale of everyday life the mainsprings of action are human emotions and personal relationships and involvements, that children feel and suffer, that realism is more than holiday expertise with boat and pony, that sticking to something that has to be done brings more satisfaction than good luck? Some of these points emerged in the first of the main history series, *In the Land of the Mogul* (1938), but they were un-

[1] R. Hoggart. *The Uses of Literacy*, Chatto, 1957.

mistakable in *Cue for Treason*, and with it a new era in the adventure story opened.

We must consider it here, for it came at a significant moment in publishing history. Basil Blackwell was anxious to raise the standard of the adventure story, and L. A. G. Strong was the editor of a series the theme of which was 'thrills and decent writing'. C. Day Lewis also wrote for this series which helped to establish the necessary adult standards. The pattern of Trease's work was gradually being defined, and before the war interrupted his progress, he had pointed the way which he and others have since followed with success.

Set in the Elizabethan period, *Cue for Treason* begins with the dramatic throwing down of a wall with which a nobleman sought to enclose the common land. The 'statesmen' of Cumberland are ranged in opposition, but unfortunately young Peter Brownrigg is detected as having thrown a rock at Sir Philip's horse. He takes to the road to escape, and later, hiding in an inn, he is carried on to the stage in a coffin in a performance of *Richard III*. There follows his association with the strolling players and Kit Kirkstone, the girl boy-player. They later join Burbage's company, work for Shakespeare and become involved in unmasking a plot against the Queen.

This book has the marks of the later mature Trease history story as well as the crowded canvas of Henty. For the first time the traditional picture of Queen Bess is linked to the fate of her subjects at the limits of her

realm in Cumberland. The songs, sonnets, dresses, play scenes are part of the real world which includes peel towers, lakes, hills and dangerous miners who are a law unto themselves. London is a fascinating but foul-smelling and dangerous place. The characters are round and full, especially the players and Boyd, the Secret Service agent. The gentle Shakespeare and the ruthless Cecil provide the shock of recognition, and the Queen is a sharp-witted old woman with a lot to worry her.

Right from the start the tale has movement, vitality and the suspense that comes from the loading of the circumstantial dice against the hero and heroine who must overcome genuine hazards with determination. The villain is more than a simple traitor, he is a usurper of rights. Trease the propagandist has now given way to the story teller who has, nevertheless, been concerned to engage our sympathies for the oppressed.

Cue for Treason showed what could be done and how children would respond. They were delighted. The task was now to consolidate the position which had been so hardly won, and the adventure story took on a new lease of life.

III. The Historical Adventure Story

The historical adventure story, that strong-featured offspring of the English romantic revival, has sometimes suffered from its great initial success. The reaction against Gothic gloom, the longeurs of Scott, the anti-romantic view of history and debunking techniques in biography, increasing diffidence about empire building, and the thorough-going new look to which useful villains like King John are subjected, all helped to make historical novels in this century a dangerous quagmire for all but the intrepid or incurable. Only Queen Elizabeth and Joan of Arc have exercised a constant lure, and the French Revolution is a necessary subject for our writers at least once a generation, as if it were a touchstone by which we tested our own security.

We have already seen the state of children's historical fiction when Trease began to write, and that *Cue for Treason* is a landmark. Now the library shelves are crowded with historical tales, and authors of distinction, Rosemary Sutcliff, Cynthia Harnett, Rhoda Power, Ronald Welch, Henry Treece, Carola Oman and others, have found in this kind the task most suited to their talents and interests. Plot there must be in the adventure story, but the old straightforward one offers too few variations, so now the writer exercises his skill in dealing with the extra dimension of historical sensibility. Gone are the days of Stanley Weyman when blocks of 'period writing' set the scene. Curiously, we are nearer

Scott than ever, for he remains, at his best, the greatest exponent of the historical novel as an organic unity.

The exact nature of the illusion is what distinguishes the novelist from the historian. In supplying books for children between twelve and fifteen, history teachers have an identity of purpose with novelists which accounts for the delight with which good new novels are greeted by the discerning, who insist that imaginative response to the past is the foundation of a historical sense. But teachers make a mistake if they expect the novelist to do all the work. Young people do not mind, in fact they enjoy, learning from story books, but they distrust lessons disguised as stories. One can be very disappointed when a conscientious and scholarly work on fifteenth century coinage fails to 'take' because the plot is too thin to carry the weight of British Museum material. The pupils' reaction will be first and foremost to the story, of which the material of history is an element, the context of the experience. The writer is not to chart the stuff of the past in an enticing order, but to communicate its felt life. His characters live not because of the authenticity of their dress, but by reason of their truth to what we know life is like.

Yet we can now recommend novels in history lessons with safety because every reputable writer takes this for granted and also subscribes to Trease's stringent demands about accuracy. Not that one cannot write an attractive historical novel without research; the evidence is all to the contrary. But it is the more authentic a work if the details are right, and there is usually no reason for mistakes. Trease himself withdrew *Running Deer* from publication after discovering historical errors committed in good faith. Details of dress, food, buildings, sleeping habits, communications are not at the forefront of the child's mind as he reads, but they stick as the whole picture is built up; they are the organisation of the illusion and take the place of metaphor, as well as giving verisimilitude to the experience. Too many dress descriptions and they will be forgotten; too much teaching about the conditions of apprentices and the story is lost. Explain where necessary, and then as part of the flow, are the conclusions to be drawn from Trease's practice. Details such as how people washed, the whereabouts of the ancient roads in England and the repercussions of the Hanseatic League are indissolubly linked with complete experience in *Word to Caesar*, where water was a problem in Rome but not in Bath, *Mist over Athelney*, with its description of the Fosseway in winter, and *The Secret Fiord*, with its particularly exciting sea adventure.

Comparisons of how authors create their reconstructions of the past suggest that the differences lie in the kind of experience they want to communicate, and here the men are distinct from the women. Miss Harnett uses detail in a meticulous way which brings alive to the senses what medieval children saw, ate, rode in, played with, so that identification is a kind of domestication of the modern child in the Middle Ages. Miss Sutcliff penetrates a period feeling by strong evocation of colour, landscape and a poetic Zeitgeist, all in a firmly-welded prose which is in itself an experience, and therefore more accessible to the brighter child. Trease uses thematic material at once clearly local and nationally significant in a swift masculine sweep of plot. He suggests that men are prepared to defend first the place where they have their roots, and in the soil of England the historical patterns persist. The theme starts locally and branches out as national interests become clear.

This is particularly so in the novels which have links with *Cue for Treason: Silver Guard*, *The Grey Adventurer*, and *Trumpets in the West*. These three stories cover the period of the seventeenth century struggle between the King and Parliament, beginning with the Civil War and ending with the advent of William of Orange. Silver Guard is the house where the earlier hero and heroine had settled down and brought up their family, who in turn have to defend it from a Cavalier's attempts to seize it. Dick Caldwell, the grey, or Puritan adventurer, seeks his fortune in the new colonies when he finds himself homeless at the Restoration. The fated Monmouth rising is seen against the lives of a group of West Country children whose choice of careers takes them to the uncertainties and glories of the London of Wren and Purcell. No one runs away to have adventures because life is boring. Instead, the heroes are set on pursuing an even course; Gervase from Boston wants to avoid the Civil War and study medicine at Oxford; Jack wants to compose. When the political situation brings upheaval they say, 'let's have it, get it over, and have a chance to think about our own business for a change'. Now, if this is a device in novel writing like any other, it also shows a change of outlook on the nature of adventure. It suggests that men are, on the whole, home-loving and peaceful, but that there are certain conditions, oppression, wrong, intolerance, under which a quiet life is impossible. The adventures are a challenge to ideas as much as a love of fighting. Very characteristic of Trease's handling of detail is the inclusion of William Harvey reading his book at the battle of Edgehill.

This group of novels carries over the social awareness of *Bows against the Barons*. The emphasis is no longer propagandist, but an attempt to put the issues fairly before coming down on one side. The Roundhead cause is made an issue of principle, not a manifestation of Puritanical ill-will. The Cavaliers are no longer the heroes, yet neither are they all silk and show. King James II has few advocates, but he is given a fairer trial than he intended for the seven bishops. The real change in the shift of power to the middle classes is seen in the motives and arguments of Dr Pharaoh, the Bunyanesque character, for whose egalitarian ideas the pillory and galley bench are the inevitable reward.

In *The Grey Adventurer* we see how attitudes grow out of a social pattern and persist after the pattern has broken down, as in the relation of master and man in the colonies and the famine that resulted from the failure to believe that the Indians could be trusted.

Without disregarding the need to present black and white issues to boys and girls, Geoffrey Trease succeeds in showing that judgment is not inherent in the events. Those who fought their king regarded it as a serious matter. Religious imposition and the conflict of conscience penetrated even the villages, and for some people, to go to America was a desperate remedy for a more desperate disease. Nor is this gloomy sociology. The vitality of youth permeates it all, and the sieges and battles have no less force and excitement for being described from the less usual (but winning!) side. Everything is not gloriously democratic in the end. 'There were a lot more rights and liberties to be fought for, undreamt of by William of Orange.'

Does it matter which side the novelist takes? Trease says it does. He adds that one must avoid 'the false general impression' which irresponsible books leave with their readers. He quotes the French Revolution as a case in point, where the English schoolboy has failed to grasp its significance for republican France because he is fed on tales of the Terror.[1] [We remember how

[1] At the time of writing this the author learned that Geoffrey Trease was completing a story of the French Revolution, *The Thunder of Valmy*.

Roosevelt's attitude to England still bore traces of his schooldays' teaching about George III.] Dorothy Neal White shows what has happened to the historical story in this respect:

'Reading a Trease story when one is an adult is mildly confusing because, vaguely remembering one's own childhood, one is surprised to find that the erstwhile "bad 'uns" have become the heroes.'

This also happens to historians and is entirely to be desired.

A different matter is the evocation of past events which sum up a whole period of vanished greatness, the large divisions of Greece, Rome and the Renaissance. What kind of an adventure did a boy have in fifth century Athens or under the Emperor Hadrian? What was England really like at the time of Alfred, that period which modern children see as a perpetual wet winter of low sunrises and great hardship with everyone living in the West of England? Trease writes here of Saxon Gloucester:

'They had taken the empty shell which Rome had left them, and filled it, not with a new city, but with a jumble of farms and cottages. Each lived inside his stockade, as though there were not friends and neighbours outside but prowling wolves of the forest. Where the ground permitted—where the spade did not yield Roman concrete, tile or brick—the Englishman made a garden or an orchard.'[1]

[1] *Mist over Athelney.*

The challenge of these periods is to localise and penetrate the glories and grandeur by the same confirmation and extension of experience, confirmation in that the hero is young, subject to the restraints of his youth and his culture, extension in that the times had a particular vitality, and were not simply a succession of 'dark ages'.

Alexis, the hero of *The Crown of Violet*, is made to go to rhetoric lessons, but he prefers to listen to Socrates whose reputation is not high with Leon, Alexis' father. The plot of this book is a carefully-woven double-stranded one, involving a Spartan conspiracy against Athens and the winning entry in the drama festival. Alexis succeeds in both fields, and Corinna finds her long-lost parents. This stretched even a willing suspension of disbelief on first reading, but the motivation is sound and withstands any hesitancy on the part of the adult reader to accept so much success. Again, the strength lies in the historical context being carried along by the action. Alexis is a gifted young poet, but he is also a boy who has to persuade his father first that he is not troublesome and disobedient. If one thinks that the adults had no chance against the children, one is reconvinced by the soundness of the events: the children are caught when they meddle, and the adults have to be consulted and persuaded before effective military action can be taken. It is an instructive exercise to knock on a plot in Trease's historical novels; they are made to withstand the carping of both children and adults.

The Crown of Violet was written after *The Hills of Varna* in which the last surviving manuscript of Alexis' play is discovered in 1509 in a Balkan monastery by Alan, a Cambridge scholar of sixteen. He is sent by Erasmus to Aldus Manutius in Venice and the tale unfolds with one adventure hard on another. Trease says of this one:

'The more I reached into the period, the more ideas came to my assistance. My youthful travellers would have to deal, I found, not only with unsympathetic and sinister monks, but with Adriatic pirates and Turkish janissaries, not to mention blood feuds in the Albanian hills. As their constant antagonist throughout the quest they had an Italian duke, one of those dog-in-the-manger bibliophiles of the Renaissance who wanted the manuscript only to lock it up in his library and deny it to the printing press. There seemed ample historical authority for the most fantastic characters and incidents I could wish to invent.'[1]

The tale has a grip of excitement from start to finish. The feeling tone in this one is memorable in that it conveys just how great was the passion for the new learning. The duke is swayed by the argument that uncorrected copies of the book would bring the new studies into disrepute. The enthusiasm of the hero and heroine for Greek books is equivalent to the present-day

[1] *Tales out of School*, p.123.

devotion to space travel, and one hopes that the keenness for the sciences will find as good an outlet in a story which conveys the authentic nature of the interest as well as this one does the lasting devotion to the classics. The character of Aldus Manutius is also excellently done. Little first-hand information is available about this printer, so he intrigues the novelist and gives him the stimulus he requires.

The same kind of feeling tone, a sense of historical period made local, comes in *Word to Caesar*, where another journey is undertaken, this time from Bath to Rome. When his father's camp is attacked, Paul, the son of a Roman legionary in Britain, escapes with the help of Severus, a Roman poet in exile. Severus has been unjustly banished and can be reinstated only if the original copy of his poem is found to acquit him of a charge of slander against the Emperor. Paul goes by ship from Arles, which comes alive as a Roman port, and the evocation of place continues strongly in the Coliseum, in the Subura, at Baiæ and the Sabine farm which had once belonged to Horace. This story has the advantage of another clearly-drawn villain. The intensity of these period tales is due in part to the embodiment of the darker side of the peaks of western civilisation in those who flourish in deceit and treachery. Men like the millionaire Calvus, the Italian duke, and the foppish Hippias show economically and clearly the forces ranged against Roman law, the spread of enlightenment and Athenian democracy.

39

To counter the emotional poverty which, he says, is 'the saddest flaw in contemporary juvenile books', Trease makes the relationship of the hero and heroine a growing one. He faces the difficulties of writing about personal relationships with tact and sense, taking refuge neither in hilarious extrovert behaviour nor in sentimentality. Jack Norwood in *Trumpets in the West* knows that a baronet's daughter will not find it easy to marry a musician, who is regarded as 'not quite a gentleman'. After their exploit as *fratres coniurati* in looking for the manuscript, Alan and Angela must go their separate ways. Paul will not settle in Bath with Julia, but finds in Tonia a friend then a wife. Adults have come to see that unless these subjects are dealt with in books written for adolescents, their sons and daughters may look for them in a less attractive form elsewhere.

The difference in upbringing between boys and girls provides a good historical 'trace'. The girls are bright, intelligent and worthy of the adventures and able to hold their own, but they are not tomboys all the time; dresses and shoes are matters of concern when they should be. Whereas the boys initiate and carry through the action, the girls deal with people and the heightened sensibility is theirs. In *Mist over Athelney*, Elfwyn, taking money from the Danes, thinks he is taking part of what they had stolen from the English. Judith rejects it: 'one part of her mind told her that it was a low form of cleverness'. Girls used to read the books their brothers brought home: now they find themselves in the adventure story in their own right. 'One has only to think of girls like Marietta Strozzi', Trease tells them, 'who broke away from her guardians at the age of eighteen, lived by herself in Florence, and had snowball matches by moonlight with the young gentlemen of that city; and Olympia Morata, who was lecturing on philosophy at Ferrara when she was sixteen.'

As the critics so anxiously remind us, the age of the hero is important. If they enjoy reading, children read books meant for twelve-year-olds at ten, and there is an uneasy probability about strenuous issues being settled by the under-elevens, however natural their inclination to escape from preoccupation with intelligence tests to detective work. The historical novel takes this in its stride; children were adults sooner in the centuries before this. The author's difficulty is to temper the realistic wind. Disasters of the kind listed in the Prayer Book are too easily found in history. It is therefore refreshing to see that when two children set out to walk from Gloucester to Chippenham in the dead of winter their first calamity is to lose their way. The heroes have the hopes and fears of adolescents. A prisoner in Arles, Paul admits that he is afraid, and his first anxiety is to save himself, but as he owes his life to Severus, he thinks it sense that he should lose it by trying to help him. Trease has shown that by admitting fear, indecision and frailty as natural, and by calling on adults to help when their action only would be effective, one increases, not diminishes, the hero's stature.

With the decline of the infant prodigy has faded the nationalist distrust of 'the foreigner'. Here again Trease is implementing his own demands. 'In so far as the story writer allows himself to introduce typical foreigners, it is up to him to see that they are closer to truth than they have been in the past.' In *The Silken Secret* (1953), set in Derbyshire with more romantic trappings than most of the earlier books are allowed, the villain is an Italian employed as a landscape gardener. He is anxious to stop the silk merchant from introducing into England the silk-throwing techniques which are the monopoly of the Piedmontese. He has family and national pride, motives which cannot be dismissed as black-heartedness. This is one of the best features in an uneven book, which has the sureness of plot and memorable characters one has come to take for granted. There is also a greater number of stock devices here than in any other, highwaymen, gypsies who poison pies, stilettos, a maze and imprisonment in a cave, as if the author were trying to show that he could use them all and still bring off a creditable historical tale up to his own standard. I find myself watching the mechanism with respect, but do not feel this one vintage Trease.

Nor is *The Barons' Hostage*, for all its appeal on Children's Hour and the support of history teachers.

It is the most overtly didactic of the historical novels, a crowded feudal scene of 1263-65 in which all is bustle, war and government. The family involvements, through which the characters shine out as of old, are complicated, and the events of this confusing time are still confusing despite the excitement of the Lord Edward's escape and the stern character of Simon de Montfort. The shape of the story is held in more closely by the record of events, and although Trease has worked his brief to give boys and girls an idea of what it was like to live at this time (this tale is in a Phoenix Book series), he is more successful when he can thread his own chain of events and use the history as context rather than plot.

The style of adventure in *The Secret Fiord*, *Word to Caesar*, and *Mist over Athelney* is characteristic of the later period. In *The Secret Fiord* Trease accepts his own challenge and introduces twins, running away, and the long-lost father, all the incidents which he has insisted are overdone in earlier children's books. Here, however, the motivation is strong enough to withstand these elements which avoid the obviousness of cliché. An unforgettable scene in a cathedral town involving the Corpus Christi play, and the escape from the Hanse merchants, show how entertainment and didacticism reinforce each other.

The apparent ease and clarity of outline of these later books owe much to the practised skill of the dialogue. This has always been the stumbling block of historical novelists whose attempts to recreate the contemporary speech of their characters is based on a mistaken imitation of the epic utterance of Meg Merrilees. A successful illusion is often disturbed by fake archaism. Trease says: 'If we accept the convention of Arabs, Eskimos and even Martians conversing in modern English, why should not Friar Tuck and Robin Hood do the same?' Another difficulty is the teachers' obsession with sentence structure. They beg children's novelists to help them in their campaign to make their pupils write in sentences. Here I urge my colleagues to give up a narrow interest for a wider one. Children must learn that there are many kinds of writing and many kinds of sentences, and if by reading Geoffrey Trease they write fast-moving dialogue, they will have learned a great deal. Also, a number of conventions have to be mastered before one is a competent adult reader, and it is just as much the function of an author to stretch his readers as to provide adequate examples of the taught grammatical rules. Dull, lifeless writing, however 'exact', is no substitute for a lively use of language.

'The two young people glanced back—the movement was instinctive, they could not help themselves. But the road behind them was an empty whiteness.

"There must be a village soon," said Elfwyn. "Keep a good look-out."

"I will."

"The very presence of those wolves is an encouraging sign——"

44

"Is it?" She was doubtful.

"Well, they're more likely to lurk round the neighbourhood where there are sheep and cattle——"

"Oh, of course. I see."

"Wolves have to live, like anyone else." [1]

To combine dialogue and description and to make both organic in a fast-moving plot is to solve the major issues of the historical novel. To do this without loss of integrity and to win the favour of the young is to earn the respect of critics, the praise of parents and the gratitude of teachers. Geoffrey Trease not only fulfils his own demands in this field but also surpasses them in giving new life to an almost outmoded *genre* which was dying for lack of conviction about the adventure of ideas. The felt life of these books is undoubted. They have the vitality and gaiety as well as the idealism and seriousness of adolescence. In respecting his audience, Trease has won for children's stories an abiding recognition they were once about to lose.

. . . . .

An epilogue on 'real history'. The story-biographies included in *The Seven Queens of England*, *Seven Kings of England* and *Fortune my Foe*, follow the prescriptions in *Tales out of School* where the author speaks with feeling of both the attraction and difficulty of writing about Raleigh and the childhood of kings and queens.

[1] *Mist over Athelney.*

Whereas the great figures of the past enter the historical adventure story to provide the 'shock of recognition', when they are the subject of study, the writer, if he is a good historian, has what George Kennan calls 'the virtue of being as close to what actually occurred as human industry and conscience can make it'. In writing history for young people, Trease steps over the line which divides what is known from what is felt, but with an integrity which illuminates rather than detracts from the importance of the facts. The facts are for the text-books, but they so rarely come alive without inspired teaching. The greatness of Raleigh is enhanced by the way he was subject to the frailties as well as the nobility of his age, and much of what Queen Mary and Queen Elizabeth did when they reigned is illuminated by their childhood restraints and fears for which the text-books have no space. These books fill the gap which separates history from life and will keep an interest alive throughout the period of wrestling with examinations.

By the time *Tales out of School* appeared in January 1949, Geoffrey Trease had established himself as a writer in almost all of the kinds of books for children which he discusses. Before 1940 came a group of plays under the title *The Dragon who was Different*, and thereafter came the historical novels which confirmed his reputation: *Running Deer*, *The Grey Adventurer*, *Trumpets in the West*, *The Hills of Varna*, *Silver Guard*. A war-time spy story, *Black Night, Red Morning*, now seems to have a topicality and fire which remind one how much easier a real enemy makes the novelist's lot. A book for backward readers (*The Mystery of Moorside Farm*) a story biography of Raleigh, a travel book and the first of the Blackwell histories had all appeared before Trease formulated his views on the position of children's authors and the books they produced. A growing body of writing for children, parental ignorance and the prevalence of the 'sensation-without-commitment' comics, as well as an undefined, generalised concern about children's reading, served to make *Tales out of School* a tract for the times.

What makes a good children's book? Trease says it is one which 'uses language skilfully to entertain and represent reality, to stimulate the imagination or to educate the emotions'. Entertainment there must be, but that will never be all, for implicit values and standards will appear in the heroes, the language they

47

use, the depth of response they call out. The adult will always include a measure of didacticism in his writing for children, if only from a conviction of his purpose. He should reinforce the work of the educationist, although the teacher will look to him not to teach the lessons, but to help the process of adjustment, which is the business of growing up.

Tales out of School suggests, in sum, that the best books for children confirm and extend the child's own experience, whether the medium be fancy, historical novel, realistic novel, story biography or school story. They all need renewed contact with life to survive, as *The Otterbury Incident* of C. Day Lewis showed in the case of the school story. The same was true of the historical novel, and in this field Trease's work stands as a considerable achievement and has made this one of the most attractive kinds of writings for both readers and authors. As for the novel of 'children just like us', Trease later attempted to put his own views into operation, with intriguing results; great popularity with children and some reservations from adults.

The strength of *Tales out of School* lies in its definition of the areas of writing for children and the standards that apply to each, all, that is, except the curious hybrid to which we have referred, the children's story which is more popular with adults. The years which have followed the publication of this book have seen an implementing of some of Trease's ideas and modification of others. But no writer now uses twins, kills off parents, sets out on a treasure hunt or engages on any domestic, scientific or fantasy pursuit without remembering that his book will have to withstand the knocking of the critics whom Geoffrey Trease has trained. The publishers have learned quickly, the librarians have a valuable ally. Teachers of teachers, whose job it is to help young adults to understand adolescents by rediscovering the child within themselves, find the difficulties inherent in the task more quickly overcome when the students read books now written for children.

And the children, what of them? It would be a poor showing if all this concern left them with their comics. Is there any evidence that it has all been worth while? Enough, I think, to be encouraging. Every time a child reads a real book instead of a comic, something has been done. The bookish children have never been so fortunate, so that one finds that those who read a great deal become discriminating sooner, although they still swallow many things at once. For young people of thirteen and over, *Enjoying Books*, written in 1952, is excellent. To review a book for children one must give them a sample, not a snippet with questions for 'comprehension'. Here is a generous measure of all kinds. Trease's favourites come off best, such as Pepys and Raleigh, but if a child has any spark at all, it will kindle at the excerpt of the Secretary of the Admiralty digging up his buried gold. *Enjoying Books* will not be chosen by children for themselves: it should be in a library where it can be put into their hands when they are wondering where to go next. Here they will find that 'what I like to read' and 'what I ought to read' are one and the same.

v. 'Children just like us'

Formula fiction pays; this is the one certain fact that emerges from a study of writing done for children. Characters in stories for the very young, produced by a mind gifted with vivid eidetic imagery and a mill-wheel industriousness, proliferate in every kind of reading format and continue their existence on cornflake boxes, soap and sweaters. However much one despises the product of 'ruthless writing down',[1] one can be roused to fury, or emulation, by the size of some royalties. The situation is made more inflammable by writers of schoolbooks who have devised formulae or teaching children to read and write without more than a passing glance at real books or genuine incentives for writing. An author's claim that he has an educational purpose, and that rewards simply come, is sometimes a rationalisation which must stand between him and an honest examination of his motives.

The critic should have an altruism the author cannot always afford, but his temptations are just as real. School stories, mysteries and fiction families are easy butts, and the substance of many a witty paragraph has come from making old-boyism, pony pranks and bachelor uncles look ridiculous in the eyes of one's fellow adults. 'A boy amongst men and a man amongst boys', they can so easily sneer at the author who, until that moment, thought he was doing an honest job.

[1] Colin Welch: 'Dear Little Noddy', *Encounter*, January 1958.

They have spent so long in being uneasily superior, these reviewers, that they ignore the need to discern a real attempt to convey experience and to distinguish it from a recipe story. A feeling that one is stooping a little is sometimes compensated for by brusque detachment. It is not easy to apply adult standards to these stories and still feel that one is making adult judgments if one does not find them immature. In making his intentions clear, Trease helps both critic and author. We shall now see how 'the changed values of the age' are reflected in the modern stories, especially those in the Bannerdale series which appeared just after *Tales out of School.*

Trease had written formula fiction long before the war. We have already seen how *The New House at Hardale* improved the stereotype but left it unchanged in outline. After this came mystery and spy stories. *Mystery on the Moors, The Lakeland Mystery, Detectives of the Dales* depart from the usual mixture by introducing real scenery and the sense of actual location which came out so strongly later in the histories and again in the post-war moderns. These mysteries were neither better nor worse than the average for the thirties, although their bulky format now looks curiously old-fashioned and they are no longer in print. I am not sorry that the brittle adult humour has gone, and that the French girl with her curious English was not thought indispensable.

The out-and-out spy story, *Black Night, Red Morning*

(1944) was allowed to lapse when it lost its topicality. The place this time is Russia, and the plot concerns the activity of Russian guerrillas against the Nazis. The urgency of war-time is on this story, and the hero is as heroic and the villain as blackhearted as one ever hopes to meet. It has dated too much to stand revival, but it has one of the most vivid of all Trease's arresting openings: 'I thought he was dead when they brought him to me. . . .'

. . . . .

Another formula is thrust upon modern authors with a plea they are expected not to resist, that they should write for young people whose reading skills are less advanced than those of their contemporaries. These unfortunates are variously called slow, backward or reluctant readers, and there is a vague generalised belief that if only they could read, many of their social adjustment problems would be solved. The situation is not so simple nor so one-sided. Backward readers are sometimes quite content with their lot; their interests are active and social, not bookish, and once they are clear of the stigma of illiteracy, it takes a very good book to tempt them away from the comic or evening paper, and an even better one to make reading a habit with its own satisfaction.

Publishers and reading experts have bludgeoned authors, but the results so far are poor. Stock situations from children's fiction with simplified sentence structure and vocabulary are the main products. Psychological jargon about reading skills conceals where the real market lies. The author has no image of the people who will read these books, the youth from the housing estate who has lost two years of school through chronic asthma, the girl whose father throws schoolbooks in the fire. There are deprived readers (no one who really enjoys reading is ever reluctant about it), who need expert help and books which reflect their interests, such as Denis Stott's Chaplinesque *Mickey Mix-up*.

As a craftsman Trease has accepted this challenge. The stories in the book called *The Mystery of Moorside Farm* are stock tales, boy and girl protagonists in adventures concerning a farm, Nazi spies, and a theatrical family. The conventions stick out, the vocabulary is simplified, but the leap to the situations of the main characters is unreal for the backward readers I know, for, more than anything else, they lack experience of storytelling. They need a different kind of illusion which gives the appearance of realism, and a quick succession of slapstick situations which produce a comic, custard-pie effect. This does not tempt the serious children's novelist. Trease's strength lies again in the dialogue. It is good that the book exists; we need so many and there are so few. A skilled author like Trease could improve on his earlier performance, but it is not easy to write effectively for the boys and girls, or rather, the young adults who appear regularly in the reports of probation officers.

. . . . .

Just after *Tales out of School* appeared *No Boats on Bannermere*. It must have been the most difficult book to write, coming hard on a definitive commitment as to what constituted the task in hand.

'When one begins to cater, like a school dietician, adding up calories and checking off vitamins, then one begins to write down.' The catering in *No Boats on Bannermere* is too efficient to make it a good book, yet it is a great favourite with children. The others in the series, *Under Black Banner*, *Black Banner Players*, *Black Banner Abroad*, *The Gates of Bannerdale*, appeared at two-yearly intervals thereafter, and have come progressively into line with the accomplishment of the historical tales. While the early ones are just as popular with the children, it is on the last two that one should make definite judgments.

They are planned and intended to be stories of children 'just like us'. They are praised by many a librarian because, as one says, the children like a story in which the characters have a complete life, 'with school, home, Scouts or any other hobbies integrated but separate themes'. They reassure readers about a world in which other children go to school (day school), play with friends, devise schemes and above all, suffer reverses and frustrations. As Trease himself says, the realisation that characters in books have the same feelings as ourselves is one of the turning points in life. In acknowledging this, the modern children's novelist has problems which E. Nesbit and Mrs Molesworth never dreamed of although doubtless they had others.

First, there is increased class consciousness, subtle yet sublimated by being discussed for weeks in the correspondence columns where the debate is overtly on the subject of the 'background' of children's books. Protests and retaliation about the middle-classness may not affect the child, but nannies and nurseries, tutors and country houses are hard to put across to children in the secondary modern. Trease is censured for making the Bannerdale children bring culture to the villages; they have a headmistress who is an expert on Viking remains and a classical headmaster of the Arnold species. The answer is not to lower one's sights about scholarship, but to make the experiences ring true so that the surroundings do not seem to be the ultimate condition of the adventure. Scholarship is much less a middle-class concern than it was.

If the problem of class must be faced, so must the modern family, with all the weight of its socio-economic implications. The family has ceased to be a group of people bound together by ties of blood and has become the unit of a culture pattern, while the critics seize on the implications of the description of every chintz cover and every tin of beans. The school is all-important for the same reason. Since 1945 the confused drive for status in the name of education has brought the public system under the gaze of bemused or indignant parents and the partisan eye of the educationists. True, many a bad book has been written about a bad school, and teachers have had to struggle against the falsehoods that have spilled over from the school story into life, but I am a little weary of the children's novel as the scrapping pitch for inadequate educational theory. Trease, following the example set by Day Lewis's *Otterbury Incident*, sends his characters to day schools, but standards of good scholarship are the same no matter where, as Mr Kingsford, the Headmaster in the Bannerdale series, would be swift to point out. The boarding schools themselves have had to give up treasure hunts these days and concentrate as much on University entrance as the rest.

On the public conscience by reason of their colourful clothes, music, restlessness and spoilt-child-ness, adolescents are anxious to define their role. Their precocity is to be understood and acknowledged rather than bewailed, and in books as well as real life this involves conflict with parents, (hitherto, as Trease reminds us, conveniently dead), developing personal relationships beyond the stage of tomboy cameraderie, and frank treatment of sexual differences. All these things, Trease says, must appear in the modern novel for children in their teens. It is a realistic demand which, if not met, will drive readers to the supplies of the newsagent and the sub-culture of the railway bookstall. Do the features of modern adolescence combine to make a good story? Is a good young citizen an acceptable hero? This is a legitimate theme and a strong one, worthy of a novelist's best intentions. The story will, however, stand or fall by its overall imaginative conviction, not by the quality of its social awareness.

The volumes of the Bannerdale series vary in effectiveness. *No Boats* sets the scene: the Melbury family, Mum, Susan and Bill inherit a cottage in Bannerdale and go there to live. Father is 'away' in Canada. He is referred to, but not hushedly, and he does not come back. His departure has left his family short of money. The friends are Tim Darren who wants to be a policeman, and Penny Morchard, whose father has a bookshop in Winthwaite, the nearest town. These are the main characters in each book together with the adults, Mr Kingsford, the Headmaster of the Grammar School, Miss Florey, the girls' Headmistress, Penny's father, the farmers, and Mr and Mrs Drake, retired actors from Sir Frank Benson's company.

To counter his own accusation that children in storybooks never grow up, Trease has taken the main four from 'eleven plus' to the career and undergraduate stage. Their adventures throughout each year are set against the normal round of term and holiday, and as GCE at 'O' and 'A' levels come in turn, so Bill and Tim, Sue and Penny rise from middle school to Sixth Form heights. Their responsibilities increase, the scope of their activities widens and their relationships deepen. The balance of home-loving Sue, motherless, harum-scarum Penny, practical Tim, and Bill the thoughtful organiser is a good one, and the reader's identification can shift from one to the other. The scenery of the lakes, the pleasant local feeling of the small town is what most children enjoy, although some in the heart of Manchester write to say that it is easy for anyone to have a good and adventurous time in the countryside.

Each book has a distinctive theme in this general background. *No Boats* sets out to make 'ordinary life meaningful and exciting', from going into a new house to discovering the ways of fell farmers. In *Under Black Banner* the friends are lost in the hills and discover a house which the War Office had requisitioned and then left to fall into disrepair. As it once belonged to the Nelsons whose son is the house sports captain, they resolve to try to win it back. Inspired by the Head's assertion that constant vigilance is the price of freedom, they set about wresting the property from the War Office, a task which moves from newspaper correspondence to tea on the terrace of the House of Commons. *Black Banner Players* introduces the two themes which persist in the later books in the series: amateur dramatics, and what the experts call 'adolescent social adjustment'. 'No girls at the Grammar' has always been Kingsford's dictum, and even although the school play is the worse for it, he sticks to his guns until Miss Florey wins him over on the score of a Christmas party in the house which serves as a field centre for both boys and girls. When the Headmaster protests, he is overwhelmed.

' "I can assure you, Mr Kingsford, it is just as irritating to me when one of my girls gets sentimental and silly

59

and I find her work suffering. But you can't prevent that sort of thing by keeping young people apart. They *will* meet, whatever their parents say—or their schoolmasters! The question is, are they to meet sensibly and naturally, as they do here, or would you rather see them mooching round the town, giggling and whistling after each other?" '

A headmistress after every girl's heart. The trouble is that since the creation of Miss Florey, the real-life ones have been more severely judged, and some still refuse to take the hint. In this book the theme of how to become an author, the right way and the spurious way, is dealt with, and Bill has a chance to show his mettle when an eighteenth century diary comes to light and its publication augments the Drakes' small pension.

The general theme of *Black Banner Abroad* is foreign travel, which includes the particular intention of seeing why it is important and exciting for the young. Recollections of school parties abroad fill the reminiscences of journalist schoolmasters and school magazines, but this tale is written from the inside of the expedition. The four friends, now the mainstay of the Black Banner Players, a company formed from both schools, have two tasks, to play *Romeo and Juliet* in a Roman theatre in Provence and to find the Frenchwoman from whom Willy the Waller stole fifty pounds just after the fall of France. The emphasis throughout is on growing personal relationships and widening experience. The book shows how, when young people go abroad, they become individuals in their own right for the first time, which is why their parents and teachers find them changed when they come back, especially if they have lived with another family. Like Bill, they may also have succumbed to the charms of Gigi, the bewitching character who, despite the author's control, nearly runs off with the story. Some of the best writing of the series is in this book; the performance of Shakespeare in the mothy dark of the amphitheatre is specially memorable. The growing awareness of deeper feelings is handled with forthrightness and tact.

Trease is always at his best when dealing with themes he cares about most. Although this is taken for granted in writing for adults, he would insist that it is also true of the children's author. The effect can be seen by comparing the earlier books with *The Gates of Bannerdale*. Scholarship, Oxford, historical research and the unforgettable performance of *The Tempest*, are the mainstay of the volume which sees Bill, the grammar school boy with National Service behind him, installed after his scholarship ordeal in the college of his choice. Penny has fought the Latin bogy and won, and now they both grow up in a different social background and move out into the world. Sue marries Johnny Nelson and Tim joins the police force, so that Mum and Miss Florey can have a rest and Kingsford moves into honourable retirement. To the uninitiated, it all sounds most cosy; to those who have sought in vain the picture of school life for the majority of boys and girls since 1945, it is quite new. And it still cannot rest there; clamour will be raised until the unmentioned thousands who have not won grammar school places have their exploits recorded. The children's novelist will not be allowed to think that his work is done just because Geoffrey Trease has brought the school and family story up to date.

Bill is the teller of the tales, and as his chronological age increases, so, mercifully, does his prose style mature. This 'young author' is an uneasy convention to which a great deal must be sacrificed, and I am sure that not enough is gained to warrant it in the early stages, for the descriptive details show the adult author's hand. Sound as the theme is, *No Boats* has a somewhat stagey plot, and the reward motif, that touchstone for all adventure stories, is a disappointment, especially after the hard hitting in *Tales out of School*. One must not be entirely swayed by the book's popularity into thinking that it is better than it is. It stretches the reader least, and this is not the kind of popularity one covets for it.

When the real difficulties of adolescents begin, when their shortcomings have to be taken into account, then Trease rises to the occasion. Bill's disappointment when he realises that his poems are acceptable only to an unscrupulous publisher, his short temper about the schemes for finding the Frenchwoman, his jealousy of Penny's unknown admirer and later of his college friend, Penny's thoughtlessness, and all their moods give the plots and themes a precision of experience which the first two lack. Sir Alfred, as one reviewer puts it, is a 'cultural villain', and the obstacles to the successful manoeuvre with the War Office are not too convincing. Everyone is so kind and helpful, so *educative*, that I am happier when we pass on to the region of conflicting emotional and intellectual drives, away from the glad animal movements.

But to emphasise the weakness would be to detract from the real achievement of the series. It has implemented the idea that 'school attendance' has become a richer thing, 'school life'. To do this, Trease suggested that 'a handful of good stories might help,' and this is exactly what he produced. Where before was a girl with a limp treated without sentimentality, or a rival tolerated because his standards of historical scholarship were sound? A boring and exasperating tutor is just as likely an inhabitant of a senior common room as a fine old scholar with great patience for the young, and the former presents the greater challenge in adjustment. The lucky accident rarely comes to the rescue of the plot, perhaps only when time and Gigi have stolen the show in *Black Banner Abroad* and the cottage has not been found. On this occasion it is worth it. Trease may not approve of the characters running away with the author, and the length of a children's novel rarely leaves room for it to happen, but this is a success. The class issue is never shirked, although it comes out most where it is most appropriate, at Oxford. The lack of money is what it always is, a nuisance.

The dialogue never really loses its sure touch, but it suffers most in *No Boats* where the curious 'simplification' is not worthy of the author's talent, and the reader is deceived by a false simplicity. I can understand a schoolmarmly complaint about this. It is much better later, but the problem of slang and the contemporary speech of the young is not yet solved; indeed it is perennial with all writers, and the adoption of a new medium, such as that used in *The Catcher in the Rye*, seems to offer a different way of going about it. That is not how adolescents actually talk, but it recreates the illusion successfully, which is better than an unreal realism. Here is Bill discussing his part in *The Tempest*.

'When I tackled him privately afterwards he said: "Look here, old chap, the voice is the main thing out there. It's no good having the daintiest ballet dancer from Sadler's Wells if the words can't be heard in the open air. You're the best we've got, so you'll have to have a shot at it."

"Couldn't you get a girl?"

"Listen," said the producer sternly, "I'm casting Ariel, not Peter Pan. Some *Tempests* have had a female Ariel but this one won't. I'm allowed to borrow girls from outside to play Miranda and the goddesses in the Masque, but I'm not having one in this part."

"But—I'll have to sing."

"Yes, you'll have to sing."

"Am I *good* enough?" I said desperately. "Some people might think I was making the most unearthly row."

"Ariel is not an earthly person, so *that* will be all right. Seriously though, Melbury—don't worry. I wouldn't ask you to do the part if I didn't think you'd be adequate. Dash it all, man, I am producing the thing. You don't suppose I want it to be a flop any more than you do?" [1]

The dialogue has to carry a firm load of description, the growth of character and more than a hint of didacticism. The pills are sometimes thinly coated, but easily swallowed. The town children must learn country ways, such as not throwing stones down potholes. With proper help the young write business letters, interview specialists, get in touch with the public services, all on legitimate occasions. They discuss careers, publishing, French food and how to order it, university and how to get in. They learn how to do research and how to behave when invited to tea (go before you're unpopular). An English master gives a lesson on Pepys that would work, all in the to and fro of speech, which represents no mean achievement, despite some reservations.

A strong sense of values is the backbone of the series. Inherited formula is made meaningful by the clash of issues and different standards of integrity, or even keeping one's self-respect. Learning about different ways of life, about knowledge, and books, all add to the interest in making normal life exciting. Teachers need no longer shake their heads over the

[1] *The Gates of Bannerdale.*

65

handling of adolescent relationships. The difference between boys and girls growing up, a feature we saw clearly in the histories, is skilfully dealt with. Here Bill shows the boy's obtuseness.

' "It's a sad case," said Mum, with something between a laugh and a sigh.

"How do you mean?"

"I suppose it's what you call in your grammar the *possessive* case. . . ." As I still stared blankly she continued. "You rather like to feel that Penny is your particular friend. . . . But you can't tie people down, Bill—least of all a person with her temperament. Possessiveness is no good, whether it's between friends of the same sex or the opposite. It's only a slightly less ugly name for jealousy."

"Oh, chuck it, Mum," I protested crossly. "I don't care twopence what friends Penny has. But she might have explained properly. It's the—the deceitfulness that gets under my skin."

"Naturally, darling, remembering the complete frank openness with which you explained your own day's doing!"

"That was different. There was a perfectly good reason why I didn't."

"Possibly *she* had one too."

. . . Mum was being, for once, unreasonable and there was no sense in arguing the point further.'[1]

No reader is deceived as to who is unreasonable.

As long as there are children's stories the adults will have to be put somewhere, so it is better if they can be

[1] *Black Banner Players.*

accepted as part of the action. They have to be revolted against; it is not fair to the children otherwise. The Melbury children grow up by having to be responsible for their mother and to see that in the lonely dales they do not have all the fun, although like a good parent she allows herself to be banished to the sales in Manchester. She plays a real adult role, not too interfering, but offering advice when asked and being firm about the social conventions which make children acceptable guests. She shows clearly what Trease meant when he said that the mortality rate amongst parents and relatives was needlessly high. The most splendid uncle cannot be expected to go on being generous at a distance.

. . . . .

Does all this add up to 'making ordinary life exciting and meaningful' by confirming what adolescents know of it and stretching their imaginations? Certainly the characters are more 'like us' than books of twenty years ago which avoided the actual situations around them. Despite claims to the contrary, I think that the good fortune of the schoolboys and girls and their adventurous situations are no more than the average child might look for these days. Perhaps the young are not always so enterprising; one could wish they were, and the interest and support of the grown-ups is more than we might be able to take for granted in many real life situations. So much the better, if children are inspired and encouraged. There is a real danger nowadays that their increased security may lessen their sense of adventure. Here as in the histories, adventure is as much the result of an enquiring curiosity and a determination to see a job through as the good fortune to be lost on the moors at night, and those who complain that it could never happen to them have not read a set of ordinary children's compositions about what goes on in the neighbourhood at weekends.

The great gap filled by these books is the one between what children read in school and what they like to read, which we mentioned at the beginning. The later volumes stretch the reader without taking him away from the security of what he knows and recognises, and increase his awareness of the value of the experience which is already his, so that his response to life and to books will deepen. The Bannerdale books are not beyond the reach of fashion; they will date more quickly than the histories, but meanwhile they offer authentic imaginative experience. Teachers who are anxious to capitalise every bit of reading done by their pupils will find that they can boost a meagre diet and at the same time discuss with the same validity the issues which emerge in weightier works. Compared with more intricately psychological children's novels (*A Hundred Million Francs*), or avowedly 'poetic' tales (*A Grass Rope*), the Bannerdale books are imaginative documentary, carrying, as their author demands that they should, the readers 'from the love of romance to the appreciation of reality'.

68

VI. Travel Fiction

'Fascinating and maddening by turns' is how Geoffrey Trease describes the mongrel art form' of the travel book written in a setting of fiction. His child heroes in 'The Young Traveller' series go to India, Pakistan and Greece with parents conveniently sent on jobs which give them a good excuse to pry around (films and university research), while to tour England in an old car they are joined by two other children from the Commonwealth who help them to see their own country with new eyes. One must remember that the intention is fact, not fiction, for the characters take an 'intelligent interest' sometimes bordering on precocity, and the quotation game can get a little out of hand in books as in real life. Adult readers are probably more sensitive to the mixture of the conventions and amazed by the amount of detail that the writer has managed to include without making it indigestible. Young readers take the setting easily for what it is, and move from sympathetic interest in the motherless son of a newspaper man to the details about the Acropolis without concern for the author, trusting that his craftsmanship will give them the interest and information they want. The facts emerge from the dialogue and from the description given by a character who has a claim to know about what he points out. For India and Greece, two places which he knows well, Trease has an unmistakable place sense which we have already seen in the novels. The historical and romantic elements which fire his imagination come out again in these books in a way which takes them out of the realms of ordinary guide books. The children note and enjoy the everyday things too, food, school, travel, as well as the special highlights of a Greek Easter and an Indian tiger hunt. All this is done with more than journalistic conscientiousness; it takes all his skill as an expert to produce a junior Baedeker.

In *The Young Traveller in England and Wales* Trease has undertaken a double task; to write for children who think they know their own country but more often do not, and for foreigners for whom the Underground and the Welfare State are as strange as the Crown Jewels. Everyone will have his own complaint about omissions, but few books are fair to Swindon and the Chalk Downs as well as to the more postcard resorts. The National Trust and the Youth Hostels' Association are just right for this stage of travelling, and one is glad to see that children are encouraged to go off before they can afford three-star hotels.

Just as Geoffrey Trease's sense of place is capitalised in these travel books, his practised hand at dialogue is in demand when we think of plays for children. There are never enough for acting in school, and teachers who have thumbed their way through countless one-act unsuitables of 'The Bathroom Door' variety are delighted with *The Shadow of Spain* where their need for many parts and sensible dialogue are efficiently met. The three plays in the book will keep the Junior Dramatic Club effectively busy and teach them a great deal about character portrayal and production. Perhaps the publishers should have issued the plays separately, as each caters for a specific classroom situation.

Dependent though he may be on the tastes and interests of the young, the children's author cannot spend all his waking hours consulting their preferences. He examines their needs, takes account of the situation we outlined at the start, but he must also enlarge their scope, and, above all, write about what *he* likes if he is to give them anything worth while. Children trust Geoffrey Trease to do this, and it is clear from the letters he receives that while they are always anxious for 'another of the same' they will accept his judgment. They ask for more Bannerdale adventures or a story of what happened to Alexis on military service. 'It is very nice', says one girl, 'to read about children you might meet in the street.' Although the letters are all responsive and grateful, they are not fulsome. The hand of the teacher who has begun to show them how to be discriminating is evident in a fair number. Some complain that it is not always possible to find all the books in the series in the library, and certainly when this study was in preparation it was impossible to rely on the local children's library for copies of the books. They were nearly always out, so they had to be tapped at the source before they reached the shelves. Publishers are hesitant to give figures and Godfrey Trease is too modest to claim how widely he is read. The librarians testify regularly to his popularity.

Children are just as anxious as adults to know how a

book is made, and they constantly ask for details and for help and encouragement in writing their own. Trease gives this picture of his background and work habits because, he says, 'I don't go in for midnight oil, temperament or self-conscious Inspiration'. Nor does he mention his infinite patience with teachers, lecturers, students and all those who take advantage of the fact that he is approachable, indulgent with his time and help, and concerned that the young should grow up into competent and sensitive readers. The secret of his work is meticulous craftsmanship and steady effort, a dramatist's eye for situation and a humanist's sympathy for his fellows. He shares with his predecessors in this series a capacity for humour and hard work.

'I now lead a quiet country life in Herefordshire. I have a pleasant little house at the foot of the Malvern Hills, with a typical English garden of very green grass and far too many weeds. My study is upstairs, with a fine panorama of the hills. My equipment is simple—a few rows of good reference books (on historical costume, social history, etc.) and a typewriter with which I write everything. I like to alternate periods of steady work with brief periods of lecturing or with journeys abroad—to collect authentic background material for some future story.'

In reply to questions about how a book comes to life he supplied these details:

'I decide on the theme—say a historical period I'm

in love with or an event which makes a good story (Athelney, Prince Edward's escape from de Montfort) and which serves as a peg for something I want to say; in these cases that Anglo-Saxon England was a civilisation and a culture, not just a rude prelude to the Normans; and that mediaeval government worked like *this* and was subject to *these* considerations. I never go just for "a good story".

'I read round the theme, trying to distil a kind of essence for the story. While reading I make pretty copious notes on costume, food, vehicles, weapons, all kinds of social history. I note, from real history, incidents and characters which can be used 'straight' or in a fictionalised form. I choose settings I already know or can visit before the book. Special points have to be checked. For the horse-doping in Queen Anne's reign I went to my brother, a professor in pharmacognosy; for inquest procedure in *No Boats on Bannermere* I attended a coroner's court: just lately I have been getting advice from civil engineers and juvenile magistrates.

'I begin to shape the story. The climax has usually been in my head from the start. The characters are gradually moulded with their names, descriptions and mental attributes, not forgetting a clear conception of their pasts and futures outside the time limit of the story. I often modify the story in many ways as I go. Fresh ideas grow out of the original stem, and some of the earlier ideas have to be cut out because there is no longer space for them. Realising how much the story does develop while I am writing I don't always wait until the plan is complete. So long as I can see the finish of the story, I may sometimes dive in before I can see the whole route. . . . My technique is pure "looking glass" . . . eat the cake first, then cut it, then bake it.

'I write the story on a typewriter. The opening pages are usually torn up and rewritten several times. After that, although I might go back and rewrite odd pages or even a whole chapter, I think that perhaps ninety per cent of my typescript used to go to the printer with no more than a few pen-and-ink cuts and alterations. Nowadays I seem to revise much more and I am very satisfied with 2,000 words on a good working day. For comparison G. A. Henty regarded 6,500 words as a good day, John Creasey (I believe) can do 11,000 in a morning. The actual writing of *The Hills of Varna* took five weeks. Nowadays with correspondence and other interruptions a similar book takes me about three months or longer. So the daily output is misleading.'

The first person to hear the story is his wife.

Translations of Geoffrey Trease's novels have appeared in French, German, Norwegian, Swedish, Icelandic, Russian, Polish, Italian, Hebrew, Japanese, and translation rights have been sold in Spanish, Portuguese (for Brazil), Dutch, Danish. This last is for *Mist over Athelney* in which the Danes are the enemy, although the heroine's good sense in choosing as her husband, not her companion of the winter journey, but a young Dane, may have contributed much to this fair-minded gesture. There have also been German language editions in Austria, Switzerland, and long ago in Russia, and separate American editions, Canadian school editions and a German school edition in English. A full length review of Trease's work appeared in Germany in 1957.[1]

Many of the translations are of the early, left-wing books. Of the mature post-war books the most popular with foreign translators are *Word to Caesar*, *The Silken Secret*, *No Boats on Bannermere*, *The Young Traveller in England and Wales* and *The Young Traveller in India*. About ten of the books have been serialised by the B.B.C. on Children's Hour, with short extracts on the Schools' programme. There have also been extracts broadcast in Canada, Australia and New Zealand.

.　.　.　.　.

The scope of this study does not include the recent adult novels—*Snared Nightingale* and *So Wild the Heart*. One cannot lay down rules for the movement of the young from juvenile to adult fiction, except to change the colour of the library ticket, but it is safe to hint that many Trease enthusiasts will have read these books before they leave school. They will find them really grown up, with new resources of wit, insight and imagination at which the children's books have already hinted, and they will not be disappointed if they look for the same enchantment.

[1] *Die Neuern Sprachen*, 12, Frankfurt, 1957.

VIII. Conclusion

Tales out of School ends with a chapter called 'To you—for action', and in the years which have passed Trease has increased the body of his work to an extent which puts him in the first category of writers for children. But more than that, he has made us all, writers, critics, teachers and parents alike, more and more aware of what is involved, and to what extent the children's writer takes on himself the task of helping to make the present generation literate. He has closed the gap between entertainment and didacticism, showing that in the children's story they merge happily together, and he has bridged the gulf between the comic and the classic in a way for which teachers can never be grateful enough. He has taught his fellow writers that if they are to earn their lauds as minor artists, only sound adult standards of integrity will do, all this with a seriousness of purpose and a sense of humour.

He will not rest on his laurels, and although the community will continue to make its demands and children to ask for another of the same he will take the lead rather than wait to be given one. The gap is now in our 'two cultures'. Our educational growing pains are not yet over as long as we have technologists who know nothing of the dreams and excitements of the period which initiated scientific enquiry, nor of Isaac Newton's preoccupation with heaven and hell. At the same time one cannot turn one's back on the atomic reactors. The children one now meets in the street are the sons and daughters of those who work there.

It is no mere extension of the habit of being, on the whole, laudatory and approving of writers of children's fiction that has produced this appreciation of his achievement. Geoffrey Trease has fully earned the status that he claims for himself and his fellow writers, and we await the results of the next twenty-five years with interest.

BIBLIOGRAPHY

BIBLIOGRAPHY

Bows against the Barons, Martin Lawrence, 1934. New edition, 1948

   The New House at Hardale, serialised in *Boy's Own Paper*, 1934, Lutterworth Press, 1953

*Comrades for the Charter, Martin Lawrence, 1934

*The Call to Arms, Martin Lawrence, 1935

    *Walking in England, Fenland Press, 1935

*Missing from Home, Lawrence & Wishart, 1937

Red Comet, Lawrence & Wishart, 1937

*Mystery on the Moors, A. & C. Black, 1937

*The Christmas Holiday Mystery, A. & C. Black, 1937, reprinted as *The Lakeland Mystery*

*Detectives of the Dales, A. & C. Black, 1938

   In the Land of the Mogul, Basil Blackwell, 1938

   The Dragon who was Different, and other plays for children, Frederick Muller, 1938

     *Such Divinity, Chapman & Hall, 1939

       After the Tempest, in *The Best One-Act Plays of 1938*, Harrap, 1939

     *Only Natural, Chapman & Hall, 1940

Cue for Treason, Basil Blackwell, 1940

*Running Deer, Harrap, 1941

The Grey Adventurer, Basil Blackwell, 1942

*Black Night, Red Morning, Basil Blackwell, 1944

Trumpets in the West, Basil Blackwell, 1947

The Hills of Varna, Macmillan, 1948

Silver Guard, Basil Blackwell, 1948

The Mystery of Moorside Farm, Basil Blackwell, 1949, for backward readers

Fortune my Foe, Methuen, 1949

The Young Traveller in India and Pakistan, Phoenix House, 1949

   Tales out of School, Heinemann, 17 January, 1949—the '1948' imprint is incorrect.

No Boats on Bannermere, Heinemann, 1949

The Secret Fiord, Macmillan, 1949

Under Black Banner, Heinemann, 1950

Enjoying Books, Phoenix House, 1951

Black Banner Players, Heinemann, 1952

The Crown of Violet, Macmillan, 1952

The Barons' Hostage, Phoenix House, 1952
The Seven Queens of England, Heinemann, 1953
The Young Traveller in England and Wales, Phoenix House, 1953
The Silken Secret, Basil Blackwell, 1953
The Shadow of Spain, and other plays, Basil Blackwell, 1953
Black Banner Abroad, Heinemann, 1954
Seven Kings of England, Heinemann, 1955
The Young Traveller in Greece, Phoenix House, 1956
Word to Caesar, Macmillan, 1956
The Gates of Bannerdale, Heinemann, 1956
      Snared Nightingale, Macmillan, 1957
Mist over Athelney, Macmillan, 1958
      So Wild the Heart, Macmillan, 1959
Edward Elgar: Maker of Music, Macmillan, 1959—in the series of
    small books for schools, 'They Served Mankind', 62 pp

  G.T. has also translated two books by René Guillot,
Companions of Fortune, Oxford, 1952 and
The King's Corsair, Oxford, 1954
    and has edited a collection of short stories,
Six of the Best, Basil Blackwell, 1955

* Out of print

AMERICAN EDITIONS OF
BOOKS BY GEOFFREY TREASE

Cue for Treason, Vanguard, 1941
The Seven Queens of England, Vanguard, 1953
The Silken Secret, Vanguard, 1954
The Seven Kings of England, Vanguard, 1955
Follow My Black Plume, Vanguard, 1963